ART IN THE AGE OF VAN GOGH

ART IN THE AGE OF VAN GOGH

Dutch Paintings from the Rijksmuseum, Amsterdam

Griselda Pollock

Alan Chong

October 24, 1998 — February 14, 1999

Art Gallery of Ontario

Toronto

FRONT COVER:
George Hendrik Breitner
Girl in a White Kimono
(Geesje Kwak), 1894 [CAT. 46]

BACK COVER:
Vincent van Gogh
Self-Portrait, 1887 [CAT. 42]

Printed in Canada

Canadian Cataloguing in Publication Data
Main entry under title:
Art in the Age of Van Gogh
Catalogue of an exhibition held at the Art Gallery of Ontario,
Oct. 24, 1998 - Feb. 14, 1999.
Includes bibliographical references.
ISBN 1-895235-95-2

1. Painting, Dutch - Exhibitions. 2. Painting, Modern - 19th century -
Netherlands - Exhibitions. 3. Haagse school of painting - Exhibitions.
4. Rijksmuseum (Netherlands) - Exhibitions. I. Chong, Alan, 1957-
II. Pollock, Griselda. III. Art Gallery of Ontario.
IV. Rijksmuseum (Netherlands).

ND647.5.H3A77 1998   759.9492'074'713541   C98-932426-5

Art Gallery of Ontario
317 Dundas Street West
Toronto, Canada
M5T 1G4 www.ago.net

The Art Gallery of Ontario is funded by the Ontario Ministry of
Citizenship, Culture and Recreation. Additional operating support
is received from the Volunteers of the Art Gallery of Ontario,
the City of Toronto, the Department of Canadian Heritage and the
Canada Council for the Arts.

Contents

OVERLEAF:
George Hendrik Breitner
The Singelbrug at the Paleisstraat in Amsterdam, 1896–98
[CAT. 47]

Sponsor's Foreword

From the elegant styles of Romanticism and Impressionism through to the sombre canvases of Modernism, *Art in the Age of Van Gogh: Dutch Paintings from the Rijksmuseum, Amsterdam* captures the beauty and influence of this unique group of artists of the Hague School. Featuring the works of Vincent van Gogh, George Hendrik Breitner, Piet Mondrian and Johan Barthold Jongkind, this collection is a premier exhibition of the nineteenth-century Dutch masters, and the first of its kind in North America since the turn of the century.

American Express is proud to be a partner with the Art Gallery of Ontario in bringing these world-renowned works of art to Canada. Well known for our sponsorship of blockbuster shows, American Express also believes that it is important that Canadians have access to a breadth of cultural and artistic experiences. For this reason, we extend our support to include anything from forming partnerships with performing arts companies, to sponsorship of local musical festivals, and funding major exhibitions at some of Canada's leading galleries.

At American Express we understand that as corporate citizens we have the responsibility and privilege of supporting and enriching the communities in which we do business. Cultural heritage projects, initiatives that address social and economic issues, and the volunteer efforts of our employees are at the heart of American Express's program of corporate citizenship.

We will continue to support arts and cultural heritage programs that touch Canadians and expose new audiences to the sights and sounds of the arts.

Alan W. Stark
PRESIDENT AND GENERAL MANAGER
AMERICAN EXPRESS

Directors' Preface

Major art exhibitions develop close ties between museums. When the Rijksmuseum decided to close temporarily its wing dedicated to nineteenth-century Dutch art, Wouter Kloek and Alan Chong, curators at the Rijksmuseum and the Art Gallery of Ontario respectively, proposed an exhibition for Toronto drawn from the rich holdings of the Rijksmuseum. The Art Gallery of Ontario is pleased to exhibit a selection of the finest nineteenth-century paintings from the collection, ranging from Romantic pictures and landscapes by members of the Hague School to the paintings of Vincent van Gogh, the Amsterdam Impressionists, and the early works of Piet Mondrian.

This exhibition focuses on some key innovative and influential developments in nineteenth-century Dutch painting. The selection of works concentrates on the experiments in light and naturalism that characterized successive generations of landscape painters. As Dutch artists began to sketch and paint out-of-doors, they rediscovered the polders, canals, windmills and villages that their predecessors in the seventeenth century had so lovingly depicted. A renewed sense of patriotism and nationalism further encouraged this pictorialism.

The exhibition also sets artists who had prominent international careers – Johan Barthold Jongkind, Vincent van Gogh, and Piet Mondrian – in their Dutch context. It examines the sources of the Hague School, its influence, as well as the rival art movements that took hold in Amsterdam at the end of the nineteenth century.

Canada enjoys a historic bond with nineteenth-century Dutch painting, and it is especially appropriate that Toronto should host this exhibition. The first art historical book written in Canada was Edward Greenshields's *Landscape Painting and Modern Dutch Artists*, published in Toronto in 1906. Canadian collectors around 1900 acquired paintings of the Hague School with great enthusiasm. The Art Gallery of Ontario has also hosted major exhibitions devoted to the art of Piet Mondrian (1966) and to Vincent van Gogh and Cloisonism (1981).

The works in *Art in the Age of Van Gogh* were selected by Wouter Kloek and Alan Chong. Guest author for this publication is Griselda Pollock, professor of art history at the University of Leeds. Maxwell Anderson, former director of the Art Gallery of Ontario, was instrumental in the early stages of developing this exhibition. We would like to thank our respective staffs who have worked with great energy to prepare and present this exhibition.

Art in the Age of Van Gogh is generously sponsored by the American Express Foundation. We thank them for their continuing support and sponsorship. The Royal Netherlands Embassy in Canada has furnished support for the publication of the catalogue.

Matthew Teitelbaum
DIRECTOR, ART GALLERY OF ONTARIO
TORONTO

Ronald de Leeuw
DIRECTOR-GENERAL, RIJKSMUSEUM
AMSTERDAM

exhibitions of modern painting became the most important venues for artists to show and sell their works.

The French abandoned Holland in 1813, and the Netherlands again became a fully independent state, with Willem I, son of the last *stadhouder*, assuming the throne as king. The cultural institutions founded by the French occupiers were retained and encouraged to flourish. A new sense of patriotism and national pride buoyed artistic activity in the Netherlands, especially in the field of landscape painting. Artists and collectors alike viewed the canals, polders, windmills and cattle of the Dutch countryside as embodying the traditional spirit of Holland, now revitalized. Favoured by Dutch artists since the seventeenth century, these subjects were now rendered with an innovative attention to the effects of light and perspective.

The cultural institutions in place by the early 1800s were essential to the growth of a Dutch school of painting. Moreover, the founding of new organizations and structures directly mirrored the changes in Dutch art in the course of the century. Nearly all of the artists represented in this exhibition trained at the national academy or at the schools that had sprung up in the major cities during the course of the eighteenth century. The national exhibitions were also crucial to Dutch artists. Around 1870, other art organizations began to hold exhibitions that greatly complicated but also significantly enriched the artistic scene in the Netherlands. The national government, on the other hand, proved a poor patron of contemporary art, while the city museums began to build their collections only at the end of the nineteenth century. Instead, an exceptionally active group of bourgeois collectors provided crucial support for Dutch painters. Almost as important were foreign clients in Britain, Canada and the United States, who avidly bought paintings of the Hague School.

A Dutch School?
All of the artists represented in this exhibition are interconnected through academies, mentors, collaborations, friendships and patrons. Even such independent Dutch painters who spent a significant portion of their career in foreign lands – Johan Barthold Jongkind, Vincent van Gogh, Lawrence Alma-Tadema and Piet Mondrian – had strong roots and connections in the Netherlands, which were never severed. Vincent van Gogh, for example, spent his early career in Holland. He was a relative and pupil of Anton Mauve and his art displays strong connections with the Hague School, which he admired immensely. Piet Mondriaan, or Mondrian as he later called himself, commenced his career as a landscape painter strongly rooted in northern

Wouter van Troostwijk
Gelderland Landscape,
c. 1809
The brilliance of sunlight
and the ordinariness of the
scene are remarkable for a
landscape of this early
date. Indeed the work pre-
dicts the developments of
the Barbizon and Hague
schools. This painting was
auctioned from the artist's
estate in 1875.
[CAT. 1]

European traditions. Although daring in composition, his *River View with a Boat* (CAT. 68) and *Farm at Duivendrecht* (FIG. 1) are essentially subjects typical of Dutch art since the sixteenth century.

Anxieties: The Past and France

For much of the nineteenth century, Dutch artists struggled with two great, but sometimes burdensome influences: seventeenth-century Dutch art and rance. Holland's great artistic tradition meant that modern Dutch painters were always compared to the painters of Rembrandt's era. Moreover, the successive waves of progressive art developments in Paris were enormously influential.

As Holland's so-called Golden Age, the seventeenth century loomed large for Dutch painters of the 1800s. The landscape and genre pictures of the past were so widely praised and so well known that they threatened to stifle inno-vation. For the most perceptive artists, seventeenth-century pictures were a source of inspiration. The new interest in naturalistic light effects of the early 1800s renewed respect for the direct compositions and clear light found in seventeenth-century landscapes. Paulus Potter's paintings of farm animals set in sunlit landscapes, for example, exerted a particularly strong influence.

FIG. 1
Piet Mondrian
Farm at Duivendrecht,
c. 1905–1907
Art Gallery of Ontario, Toronto

13

Wijnand Nuyen
Shipwreck on a Rocky Coast,
c. 1837
Nuyen's dramatic colour
and brushwork were strongly
influenced by Eugène Isabey
and Richard Parkes
Bonington. This work
belonged to King Willem II
and was auctioned with his
entire collection in 1850.
[CAT. 4]

The successive forces of French Romanticism, Realism, Impressionism, Post-Impressionism, and Symbolism threatened to overwhelm Dutch painting. This naturally led to a sense of independence if not determined resistance to French art. As devices and techniques were borrowed from France, many Dutch artists continued to treat the subjects perfected by their Dutch seventeenth-century forebears: canals, windmills, villages and farms.

The exhibition commences with a remarkable landscape by Wouter van Troostwijk, a simple rural view in the eastern Netherlands marked by an intense sunlight (CAT. 1). The painting was made around 1809, when the French still occupied the Netherlands, and is a precocious combination of brilliant illumination, a deep forest scene, and a straightforward composition – effects that the French Barbizon School would develop only decades later. If not actually painted out-of-doors, the picture possesses a strong sense of nature observed. Equally notable for its strong light is the panorama painted by P.G. van Os in 1818 (CAT. 2). While the anecdotal details and the precision of detailing hark back to traditional compositions, the abruptly cut-off view and the sunlight reflected in the waterway point the way to the future. An artist

J. H. Weissenbruch
View near the Geestbrug:
The Rijswijk Shipping Canal,
1868
[CAT. 22]

of the following generation, J.H. Weissenbruch crafted a picture of almost identical components: a waterway diagonally splitting the scene and a view down onto a simple country lane (CAT. 22). While some landscapes produced in the Netherlands have a Romantic sensibility (CATS. 4, 6, 8), many Dutch paintings from before 1850 have a strong sense of independence.[1]

The Hague School

Influenced by the activities of French painters at Barbizon, artists began to gather at the village of Oosterbeek in the eastern Netherlands to paint out-of-doors. Sometimes known as the "Dutch Barbizon," this circle of artists encouraged the formation of other organizations of artists. Around 1870 several painters began to work together informally in The Hague, eventually becoming a close community of artists. The group included natives of the town and a few regular visitors, but many key members – H.W. Mesdag, Jozef Israëls, Jacob Maris and Anton Mauve – moved to the city between 1869 and 1871. In 1875 a critic coined the term "the Hague School" to describe this group. Their subjects included both traditional farm landscapes and depic-

15

FIG. 3
Vincent van Gogh
*A Woman with a Spade,
Seen from behind,* 1885
Art Gallery of Ontario, Toronto

tions of peasants and fishermen. The group's use of grey tonalities and deliberately moody atmospheres excited much comment and ensured their commercial success.

Rural labourers formed a major theme for Hague School painters. Jozef Israëls created a moving series of paintings that depicted the tragedies and hardships of those who worked on the Dutch coast. Anton Mauve painted various rural labourers, including woodcutters who eked out an existence in the eastern Netherlands (FIG. 2). Vincent van Gogh's depictions of peasants (FIG. 3) were influenced both by French painters such as Jean-François Millet and by Mauve and Israëls. Jacob Maris also succeeded in capturing the hardship of daily life in the impoverished countryside through an innovative landscape composition (CAT. 33, REPRODUCED ON p. 60). His truncated windmill captures the dreary and sombre life of the people of the land. A peasant woman trudges over a bridge, the top of the mill cut off from her – and our – view. The other version of the scene with the complete windmill (FIG. 4) presents a more optimistic view.

The painters of the Hague School sought an organizational structure to further their activities. Most of the group joined the Pulchri Studio, a self-governing artists' society that had been founded in 1847, and which furnished a lively forum for the group. Later in the century, Pulchri held annual exhibitions. Because many of the artists also worked extensively in watercolour, the Dutch Drawing Society (Hollandsche Teeken-Maatschappij) was founded in 1876. Dutch art dealers also encouraged the artists to work and exhibit together, so that their work could be more easily marketed abroad as "the Hague School."[2]

Amsterdam in the 1880s and 1890s

A remarkable shift in Dutch art occurred in the 1880s as experimentation migrated from The Hague to Amsterdam. Where the Hague School had favoured rural themes, a new generation began to concentrate on the urban environment. It is no coincidence that these painters were based in Amsterdam, a newly burgeoning metropolis, rather than The Hague and its surrounding hamlets. George Hendrik Breitner, in particular, espoused a philosophy that echoed the French Impressionist credo of the modern painter "to be a painter of the people." He painted the profound changes that industry, trade and construction brought to the city of Amsterdam. Breitner was a decisive influence on several other painters including Isaac Israëls (son of the famous painter Jozef Israëls), Willem Witsen and Willem de Zwart. These painters of modern life in the city became known as the Amsterdam Impressionists. They also sought institutional legitimacy by joining the avant-garde literary movement called the *Tachtigers* (Eighties Movement), which also furthered the cause of the painters.

The Rijksmuseum and 19th-Century Dutch Painting

The Rijksmuseum was founded in 1800 under a plan devised by occupying French forces. The art collection of the last Dutch *stadhouder*, Prince Willem V, was sold or taken to Paris as war booty. The remaining objects were gathered together in the Huis ten Bosch, a small palace just outside The Hague. Called the National Art Gallery (Nationale Kunst-Gallery), this new national museum opened to the public in May 1800. In 1808 the collection, now called the Royal Museum (Koninklijk Museum), was installed on the second floor of the seventeenth-century Town Hall in Amsterdam, then used as a residence by King Louis Napoleon.

Although most attention was focused on acquiring seventeenth-century Dutch paintings, the idea gradually evolved that the museum should also collect contemporary Dutch art in order to prove that the achievements of the national school did not end with the death of Rembrandt. This echoed the German concept of a "national gallery," which was devoted exclusively to contemporary art of the native country. In 1838 the Dutch government decided to establish a separate national museum of modern art in Haarlem (Rijksverzameling van Moderne Meesters). In 1885 the present building of the Rijksmuseum was completed, and the old master and contemporary components were reunited. Designed by P.J.H. Cuypers, the vast, imposing structure emulates the architecture of the sixteenth and seventeenth centuries (FIG. 5).

The core of the Rijksmuseum's collection of Dutch nineteenth-century art is composed of a gift by J.C.J. Drucker and his wife Maria Lydia Fraser. Drucker was born in Holland but set up his business in London, where he married. The couple had avidly collected paintings and watercolours by living Dutch

FIG. 5
The Rijksmuseum, Amsterdam
P.J.H. Cuypers, architect

Johan Barthold Jongkind
View on a French River, 1855
[CAT. 9]

artists, and beginning in 1909, gave portions of their collection to the Rijksmuseum. In order to display this important new gift, known as the Drucker-Fraser collection, a new wing was built in 1916. Other private collectors have enriched the collection, especially J.B.A.M. Westerwoudt of Haarlem, and the Amsterdam diamond merchant Andries van Wezel.

Renovation of the nineteenth-century wing, completed in 1996, signals that the national collection of the Netherlands must include prominent representation of Dutch nineteenth-century painting, confirming it as a legitimate successor to the Golden Age, and equally worthy of study and appreciation.

The Market for Dutch Painting in North America 1870−1915

The United States and Canada were crucial to the commercial success of Dutch nineteenth-century painting and in an important sense, the Hague School would not have flourished in the manner it did without the large number of wealthy patrons in Great Britain, Canada and America. The first Dutch painter to capture the fancy of North American collectors was B.C. Koekkoek. Edward Strahan's survey of North American collections, published in 1880, reveals a significant number of paintings by Koekkoek, but only single works by J.B. Jongkind, Matthijs Maris, Lawrence Alma-Tadema, and, remarkably, a rare work by Wijnand Nuyen.

18

B.C. Koekkoek
Winter Landscape, 1838
This painting formed part
of the important collection
assembled by the Amsterdam
banker, Adriaan van der
Hoop. In 1854 the collection
was bequeathed to the city,
and in 1885 placed on
permanent loan to the
Rijksmuseum.
[CAT. 5]

The great period of collecting Dutch nineteenth-century painting began around 1900, when the Hague School became tremendously popular in America and Canada. There were probably more significant collectors of Hague School art in Montreal than anywhere else, William Learmont and Sir George A. Drummond being perhaps the most active collectors. Another important collector Edward B. Greenshields wrote a highly personal history of the Hague School in 1906, which was the first art historical work published in Canada.[3] So popular did Dutch artists become with Montreal collectors that Canadian painters, perhaps understandably, grew resentful. The painter A.Y. Jackson complained:

> It was boasted in Montreal that more Dutch art was sold there than in any other
> city on this continent. Dutch pictures became a symbol of social position and
> wealth. It was also whispered that they were a sound investment. They collected
> them like cigaret cards. You had to complete your set....The houses bulged with
> cows, old women peeling potatoes, and windmills....They were grey, mild, inoffen-
> sive things, and when surrounded by heavy gold frames covered with plate glass
> and a spotlight placed over them, they look expensive.[4]

The reasons for the popularity of the Hague School in the United States and especially Canada are not immediately obvious. Some observers have suggest-ed that the sombre landscapes and highly emotional figural scenes were

19

Willem Maris
Cow Reflected in Water,
c. 1885–95
The subject of the painting
was one of the artist's
favourites. He wrote, "I don't
paint cows, I paint the
reflections of light," and
indeed Willem Maris generally avoided the misty grey
colouring favoured by most
of the Hague School.
[CAT. 35]

bought by collectors who lived in similar settings such as Scotland and
Canada. While Scottish-Canadians may have been influenced by the initial
popularity of Hague School painters in Britain, the general success of the
school in North America is probably linked more generally to their broad
appeal to bourgeois collectors and their compatibility with the even more
popular landscapes of the French Barbizon painters. Without doubt, Barbizon
pictures and Hague School works were collected in tandem since their subjects and techniques were similar.

The most popular Dutch artists in North America were Jozef Israëls, Jacob
Maris and Anton Mauve, followed closely by Willem Maris, H.W. Mesdag and
J.H. Weissenbruch. Paintings by Vincent van Gogh were much slower to
appear in American collections than in comparable German and French collections. Dr. Albert Barnes was the first to acquire paintings by van Gogh,
when he bought two portraits in 1912.[5]

In the 1920s, the demand for Dutch nineteenth-century painting began to
decline sharply, with the notable exception of works by Vincent van Gogh,
whom dealers could now group with the French Post-Impressionists. In suc-

ceeding decades, Dutch nineteenth-century art drifted into almost total obscurity as Hague School paintings were consigned to museum storage vaults and frequently de-accessioned. Today only a handful of Hague School pictures are displayed in public institutions in North America. Only in the last few years has the market value of nineteenth-century Dutch painting slowly increased, stimulated by new generations of collectors based particularly in the Netherlands. As the art of van Gogh becomes ever more fascinating to scholars and museum-goers, perhaps attention will also turn to his compatriots who shared so many of his interests.

NOTES

1. On the issue of Romanticism in the work of Wijnand Nuyen and Johannes Tavenraat, see Louis van Tilborgh, "Dutch Romanticism: A Provincial Affair," *Simiolus* 14 (1984): 179-188.
2. See Dieuwertje Dekkers, "Where Are the Dutchmen?: Promoting the Hague School in America, 1875-1900," *Simiolus* 24 (1996): 54-73. Beginning with the 1876 World's Fair in Philadelphia, where numerous modern Dutch paintings were exhibited, Dutch dealers attempted to promote the Hague School in the United States.
3. *Landscape Painting and Modern Dutch Artists*, Toronto, 1906. In 1904 Greenshields had written a book about Weissenbruch, *The Subjective View of Landscape Painting, with Special Reference to J.H. Weissenbruch from Works of His in Canada*. On Canadian collecting of the Hague School, see Marta Hurdalek, *The Hague School: Collecting in Canada at the Turn of the Century* (exhibition catalogue) (Toronto: Art Gallery of Ontario, 1983).
4. A.Y. Jackson, "If Cow Can Stay in Parlour, then Why Can't Bull Moose?," *Toronto Star*, 27 February 1925; quoted in Peter Mellen, *The Group of Seven* (Toronto: McClelland and Stewart, 1970): 5.
5. *Portrait of the Postman*, De la Faille, 1970, no. F435; *The Smoker*, De la Faille, 1970, no. F534; Barnes Foundation, Merion, Pennsylvania.

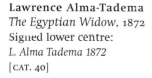

Lawrence Alma-Tadema
The Egyptian Widow, 1872
Signed lower centre:
L. Alma Tadema 1872
[CAT. 40]

The Cities and Countries of Modernity

Van Gogh among His Dutch Contemporaries

GRISELDA POLLOCK

> *Therefore, speaking only from an artistic point of view, I tell you that
> in my opinion you as a Dutchman will feel most at home in the Dutch intellectual
> climate, and will get more satisfaction from working after the character of this
> country (whether it be figure or landscape) than specializing in the nude. ...And as
> I see it, both you and I cannot do better than work after nature in Holland, land-
> scape or figure. Then we are ourselves, then we feel at home, then we are in our
> element. The more we know of what is happening abroad, the better, but we must
> never forget that we have our roots in Dutch soil.*
>
> – VINCENT VAN GOGH TO ANTON VAN RAPPARD, 15 OCTOBER 1881[1]

Art history leads us into bad habits. We use the famous – Vincent van Gogh
or Piet Mondrian – to solicit an appreciation of their unjustly neglected or
lesser known Dutch predecessors and contemporaries in the Hague and
Amsterdam schools (1870–1910). At first sight, it might seem hard to accommodate so adamant a statement of national affiliation – rootedness in Dutch
soil – as van Gogh made in his letter to his friend and fellow artist Anton van
Rappard, with the popular idea that van Gogh was one of the French Post-
Impressionist quartet. Van Gogh, along with Seurat, Gauguin and Cézanne,
have been conventionally positioned as the founding fathers of international
Modern Art.[2] We shall have a less mythical understanding of van Gogh's work
and career by allowing his Dutch origins and the rich cultural context of thir-
ty-three of his thirty-seven years to be acknowledged as one of the most pro-
foundly formative influences on the art we know as "van Gogh."

A broadened approach to the diversity and variety of artistic cultures in
nineteenth-century Europe and the United States and Canada, however,
allows us not only to see the context out of which the canonical few emerged,
but to appreciate how shared concerns with the problematics of modernity
were played out in different ways in the representation of city and country
over the nineteenth century. A thematic approach becomes necessary if we
wish to move beyond a lexicon of named artists, biographies and stylistic
histories of art that reproduce only a selective canon.

Anton Mauve
Morning Ride on the Beach,
1876 (detail)
[CAT. 28]

23

During the nineteenth century, the Netherlands – founded as a nation composed of seven provinces in 1609 after the religious war of independence from Spain – was a society in social and economic transition. While belatedly undergoing industrialization in the 1870s, the country was also being reshaped by its aggressive colonial interests in what is now Indonesia and the West Indies. Such structural changes also effected consciousness and culture, producing overt political conflict around the extremes of urban and rural poverty and the excesses and abuses of colonialism.3 What occurred in specifically artistic and literary circles was a shift from a Romantic view of nature's dramas or a lyrical appreciation of the traditional forms of Dutch landscape and city view (CATS. 1, 6, 19) toward a more observed and critically studied representation of the cities and countrysides under a Naturalist aesthetic (CATS. 33, 50, 54, 60). This change registers the impact of what we call modernity, a kind of self-consciousness and even anxiety about the character, meaning and effects of the radical changes resulting from industrialization, a new kind of urbanization and the forming of "New Worlds" in the United States, Canada, and European colonies worldwide.

In order to extend our understanding of what occurred in the nineteenth century – in Canada as much as in the Netherlands – we shall need to look beyond the modernist story of art that has focused so exclusively on what happened in the French capital, Paris, and then New York. Van Gogh and Mondrian become significant in a new way as artists who bridged several art worlds and thus force us to approach art's histories from a perspective that can include The Hague or Amsterdam as much as Paris. Van Gogh was born and worked in Holland until 1885 (apart from short periods when he was employed in the art trade in London, 1873–75, and Paris, 1875–76); he moved to Paris in 1886 and remained in France where he died in 1890 in Auvers-sur-Oise. Piet Mondrian, born Mondriaan in 1872, was trained to draw and paint by his artist father and uncle, both inhabitants of The Hague, the artistic centre of the Netherlands at the time. He remained in Holland until his first trip to Paris in 1911, returning there again only in 1918. He eventually left for New York in 1940 to escape the German invasion. What made it possible for both these artists to move from the domestic art worlds and national cultures in which they were educated and trained to participate in an international movement called Modern art was the particular and distinctive developments at home of trends that would be echoed in different ways in other artistic capitals – Paris, London, New York, Berlin or Toronto. To garner the full richness of cultural responses to

Willem Roelofs
Landscape with Approaching Storm, 1850
The work was painted in Brussels a few years after the artist moved there from The Hague, and just before his visit to Barbizon.
[CAT. 19]

George Hendrik Breitner
The Damrak, Amsterdam, c. 1903
After 1900 Breitner painted calm views of Amsterdam, which are almost devoid of figures.
[CAT. 50]

Vincent van Gogh
Village at Sunset, 1884
This landscape was painted in May 1884 in Nuenen.
[CAT. 41]

Piet Mondrian
River View with a Boat, c. 1903
[CAT. 68]

modernity, therefore, we must do more than cast a casual glance at the apparent byways and margins of the mainstream stories of art. We need to make efforts to seek deeper understanding of the many cultural streams that collectively create the complex fabric of art's histories.

With their own experience of the distorting effects of American and European hegemony, Canadians will hardly need to have underlined the need for a broader, more comprehensive and differentiated picture of the historical kaleidoscope of cultural change and artistic practice. These may, at root, share common problems across many countries, like modernization and its diverse cultural effects on the ways of understanding community, nationhood, individuality, the land and social life. Nonetheless, there were significant local differences. Using the internationally known and thus uprooted, de-nationalized modernist heroes like van Gogh and Mondrian to introduce the extraordinary diversity and interest of their Dutch contemporaries, from whose practices they themselves derived their own artistic programs, is a major contribution to the struggle against a narrowly canonical Modernism and the battle for enlarged and more historically sensitive histories of art.[4]

Challenging the Canon: Not only Dutch, but Women, too

This expanding appreciation of Dutch nineteenth-century painting is also being internally revised by a fuller appreciation of the contributions of its many artists who were women. Suze Bisschop-Robertson was much admired by Piet Mondrian for her bold and expressive use of impasted paint. Her *Head of a Peasant Woman* (FIG. 1) dates from the mid 1880s, the time when Vincent van Gogh, calling himself "a painter of peasants," was also exploring the relations between a heavily loaded brush, earthy colours, and the harsh conditions of rural life reflected in the faces of prematurely aged peasant women that he would incorporate into his *The Potato Eaters*, 1885 (Rijksmuseum Vincent van Gogh, Amsterdam). This work aligns van Gogh with a major interest among Dutch painters in issues of labour and the rural poor, represented for instance by Jozef Israëls.

Thérèse Schwartze was one of the best known and internationally reputed portrait painters of her generation, a position that made her extremely wealthy. She had studied in the major art centres of Munich (1875–77) and Paris (1879, and again in 1884); she exhibited at the Paris Salon and at international exhibitions, where her work was awarded gold medals. Her striking *Self-Portrait* of 1888 was acquired by the Uffizzi Gallery in Florence (FIG. 2).

Thérèse Schwartze
Portrait of Lizzy Ansingh, 1902
[CAT. 64]

FIG. 2
Thérèse Schwartze
Self-Portrait
oil on canvas
Galleria degli Uffizi, Florence

Her *Portrait of Lizzy Ansingh*, 1902 (CAT. 64) is a fine example of Schwartze's broad painterliness and sense of drama as a figure painter. She defies mere pretty stylization of Woman in a strikingly modern homage to the seventeenth-century Dutch portraitist Rembrandt, whose brooding self-portrait with cast shadows and masterful use of the loaded brush is deployed to introduce the viewer to the image of another artist, Schwartze's niece, who, with her, belonged to a renowned group of women artists active in Amsterdam at the turn of the century, known as the *Amsterdam Joffers*, or Damsels.[5] These images of women by women are symptomatic of modernity, which both opened up opportunities for women professionally while also making the representation of woman a major cultural question.[6]

29

Jan Veth
Cornelia, Clara, and Johanna Veth: The Artist's Three Sisters, 1884
Jan Veth painted this portrait while he was still a student
at the academy in Amsterdam. He kept this intensely moving
and personal portrait his entire life.
[CAT. 63]

George Hendrik Breitner
Girl in a White Kimono (Geesje Kwak), 1894
Like many artists across Europe in the late nineteenth century, Breitner was fascinated by things Japanese.
In 1892 he saw an exhibition of Japanese woodcuts and shortly thereafter embarked on a series of photographs
and paintings of young women dressed in kimonos. The carpet, sofa and screen form an overall decorative
ensemble. The model in this painting was the 16-year old Geesje Kwak, daughter of a local milliner.

[CAT. 46]

FIG. 3
George Hendrik Breitner
The Singelbrug at the Paleisstraat in Amsterdam, 1896
photograph of original composition

Singelbrug at the Paleisstraat

A different view of modern woman is both theme and problem in the work of one of the most notable of the late nineteenth-century Dutch modernists, who fully deserves international recognition, George Hendrik Breitner. His *Singelbrug at the Paleisstraat in Amsterdam*, 1896–98, (CAT. 47) is typical of Breitner's engagement with modern urban life. Originally painted in 1896, the canvas underwent radical changes in 1898 in order to accommodate public sensibilities around gender and public space. Breitner's painting shares a modernist syntax – a mixed crowd of workers and bourgeois glimpsed on the street – with the most advanced of Parisian paintings like Gustave Caillebotte's *Pont de l'Europe*, 1876 (Musée du Petit Palais, Geneva), which was exhibited at the 1877 Impressionist exhibition, and Edgar Degas's "snapshot" effect of partial figures pinned up against the surface of the canvas in his *Place de la Concorde (Vicomte Lepic and His Daughters)*, c. 1875 (recently rediscovered in Russia). Breitner's cropping of the foreground figure may be derived from his daring incorporation of the unexpected effects of photography, which he also, like Degas, practised. Such casual informality, typical of the street photo of figures walking towards the photographer, would, however, have a very different impact – and morality – in a large-scale oil painting.

32

George Hendrik Breitner
The Singelbrug at the Paleisstraat in Amsterdam, 1896–98
In 1896 the manager of the Van Wisselingh Art Gallery suggested
that Breitner repaint the central figure to change her from a
street girl into an elegantly dressed lady.
[CAT. 47]

Breitner's 1898 version of the painting places the viewer in a sudden,
unmediated encounter with a fashionably dressed, veiled woman. We are
almost face-to-face. Her clothes indicate her class, or do they? Is she a member
of the bourgeoisie or a fashionably kept woman? The ambiguity renders the
proximity all the more daring and provocative. Yet her veiled face and her
fur-trimmed pelerine – detailed with the same passion as Édouard Manet
expressed for women's *haute couture* – renders her Modern Woman, an image
of mystery and protected allure. [7] In the original painting of 1896, however,
known to us through a photograph (FIG. 3), the foreground female figure was
adamantly working class, unhatted, bare-faced, and behind her were other
working women, servants and waitresses, whom Breitner replaced in 1898
with more reassuring groupings of a family (on the left), a mother and child
(left middle ground), and a bowler-hatted man (on the right) screening the
two working women (CAT. 47).

In the original street scene, the viewer thus encountered, with a photo-
graphically shocking directness, the space of imagined cross-class and cross-
sex exchange; the viewer was presumed to be, like the artist, a bourgeois
man. Indeed, this is the same space of sexual fantasy and commodification

Isaac Israëls
A Shop Window, c. 1894–98
[CAT. 54]

Willem de Zwart
Hackney Coaches, c. 1890–94
This depiction of horse-drawn cabs in The Hague waiting in the rain was produced during de Zwart's sojourn at the Loosduinen artists' colony.
[CAT. 60]

as Manet distilled into his exemplary statement about metropolitan modernity, *Bar at the Folies-Bergère,* 1881–82 (Courtauld Collection, London), which also precipitates the viewer into an ambiguous exchange with an impassive woman.[8]

Breitner's modifications, however, shifted the painting's range of meaning toward the mixing of class in a public space charged with Baudelairean dreams of the encounter with an enigmatic, but forever unknown Woman. In his study of the French poet Baudelaire, the metropolis and modernity, Walter Benjamin analyzed Baudelaire's poem "A Une Passante" (To a Lady Passing By), arguing that its evocation of the flâneur's momentary glimpse of a beautiful woman soon lost in the crowd revealed "the function of the crowd not in the life of the citizen, but in the life of the erotic person"; and that "the delight of the citydweller is not so much in love at first sight as love at last sight."[9] Benjamin stressed both the masculine erotics of public spaces in the modern city and the way that this juxtaposition of the intimate and the impersonal – the possibility of feeling aroused or disturbed by a sudden interruption of one's own consciousness by the unknown others – creates an aesthetics of shock. George Breitner's paintings of the self-con-

George Hendrik Breitner
Ships in the Ice, 1901
[CAT. 49]

sciously modernizing city of Amsterdam in the 1890s offer their own singular pictorialization of this key Baudelairean trope. Deeply involved in photography, Breitner used it as a distinctly modern aesthetic resource for a new syntax for painting to distill this "shocking" quality of street life – casual, unforeseen, indifferent, full of the mystery of who the other is and why they are there, offering the possibilities of encounter and disappointment at missed opportunities, and, above all, revealing ambivalence towards the status of women who used public space for work, shopping or leisure in a culture that made the street the real and imaginary domain of men.[10] In a study of Breitner's photographic work, Tineke de Ruiter contrasts the artist's formalist exploration of the geometry of Amsterdam house architecture, the canals and barges, often redefined by snow, with his flâneur's fascination with the casual mobility of crowds on the streets. She frames the differences as the tension between dynamism and stillness.[11]

Willem Witsen
Winter Landscape, c. 1895
The work was painted at Ede,
a village in Gelderland in the
eastern Netherlands. The
composition borders on the
abstract but also possesses a
strong, palpable mood.
[CAT. 57]

Dynamism and Stillness: Two Responses to Modernity

Dynamism and stillness could be used as the polarities with which to consider the whole range of work in this exhibition. Each pole could be seen as one response to the changes wrought by modernization of city and country, identity and consciousness, social change and natural order. The nineteenth-century artists who most distinctively created a new image of the Dutch landscape tend to stress the stillness of a well-regulated agricultural landscape bathed in the warming light of a Northern summer (CATS. 11, 38). In winter scenes (CATS. 5, 45, 57) also immensely popular, the blanket of snow and frost-covered trees were used to produce a pictorial unity that evokes the sound-damping stillness of pristine winter mornings. The distinctive feature of the Hague School painters can be discerned in their preference for a compositional format that stresses repeating horizontals.

The flatness typical of Holland's polder landscapes presents considerable challenges to landscape artists, precisely because of its own uneventful planarity. Early in the century, Romantic painters invented incident out of

37

Jan Toorop
The Sea at Katwijk, 1887
Painted entirely with a palette knife, this seascape is an
early work made in Brussels. It shows the influence of H.W. Mesdag
but also of the late seascapes of Gustave Courbet.
[CAT. 66]

Gerrit Willem Dijsselhof
Tulip Fields, c. 1905
[CAT. 62]

Willem Roelofs
Meadow Landscape with Cattle, c. 1870
Painted just around the time the Hague School was formed, this landscape clearly shows characteristics of the new movement.
[CAT. 20]

dramatic weather conditions and tortured, windswept bushes. From Mauve to Maris and Weissenbruch and onto Witsen, from oil to watercolour, we find a new vocabulary emerging to meet the challenge of the low horizon, the fore-shortened recession of rectangles of orderly fields, and of finding a composi-tional formula for flat land, lots of sky and the odd windmill.[12] The effects were so tranquil – images of almost impenetrable calm, yet so eloquent of a created and managed agricultural order – that we can begin to understand the enormous success of the Hague School landscape painters, whose major international collectors in Britain, Canada, Germany and the United States were often industrialists and especially railway engineers. Their boardrooms and drawing rooms from Scotland to Illinois were decorated with this con-structed vision of Holland's profound but fertile stillness.[13]

At the same time, the formal shapes of built environments in the old urban centres of the Netherlands could offer images of timeless stillness – as in Cornelis Springer's evocation of the past in *View of The Hague from the Delftse Vaart in the Seventeenth Century*, 1852 (CAT. 7) or Willem Witsen's juxtaposition of commercial buildings with the traditional Dutch drawbridge and canal system in *Warehouses on the Uilenburg, Amsterdam*, c. 1911 (CAT. 59). On the other hand, this same urban architecture could signify change and transformation, as they did in Breitner's studies of construction sites (CAT. 48), where the disorder of the torn-down and the not-yet-built provoked interesting compositional solutions to the problem of representing disorder without producing a chaotic, illegible picture.

Dynamism, representing the conflicts of change against stillness, and a longing for continuity echo the compulsions of modern painting that must create a pictorial order while creating a vocabulary through which to register the transformations we call Modernity. In this struggle, George Breitner stands out as the central figure; the difference of his work in the city from his predecessors' images of rural or old civic Holland enables us to define more clearly the differing conceptions of painting and formal solutions between the major Dutch schools of the second half of the nineteenth century.

Willem Witsen
Warehouses on the Uilenburg, Amsterdam, c. 1911
After 1902 Witsen painted the warehouses and industrial buildings along Amsterdam's canals. In 1910 he bought a small boat from which to paint, and it is very likely that this work was made on the water.
[CAT. 59]

Cornelis Springer
View of The Hague from the Delftse Vaart in the Seventeenth Century, 1852
The painting is a model for a much larger painting made by Springer in collaboration with Kasper Karsen (also in the Rijksmuseum) for Rembrandt festivities held in 1852. The large panorama was one of 28 paintings that depicted scenes from the 1600s and decorated a large hall in Amsterdam.
[CAT. 7]

George Hendrik Breitner
*Midday Break at a Building
Site on the Van Diemenstraat,
Amsterdam*, c. 1898
[CAT. 48]

FIG. 4
George Hendrik Breitner
The Soup Kitchen, c. 1882
Stedelijk Museum, Amsterdam

Breitner, van Gogh and the City

Since enrolling in the Academy in The Hague in 1876, Breitner lived and
worked in the traditional royal capital of the Netherlands' which was famous
for its beautiful canals, grand houses and surrounding woods. Rather than
painting these picturesque aspects, Breitner was much inspired by the then
shocking modernity of French Naturalist authors, Emile Zola and de
Goncourt brothers, whose novels used new sociological techniques of social
observation and data collection to introduce into literature the darker
aspects of contemporary city life in Paris. They focused on the city's working-
class districts, where hardship and poverty leading to drink and prostitution
vied with struggles to maintain personal dignity and family coherence. The
sense that modernity would be captured by closer study of the city's shifting
populations had also produced the London novels of Charles Dickens, so
admired by Vincent van Gogh. The artist arrived in The Hague in December
1881 to study with his cousin by marriage, the landscape painter Anton
Mauve. Although van Gogh saw the works of the major artists of the group
that had since 1875 been known as the Hague School at exhibitions and
through visits to studios, his personal awkwardness and lack of mastery of

FIG. 5
Vincent van Gogh
The State Lottery Office, October 1882
Van Gogh Museum, Amsterdam

FIG. 6
Vincent van Gogh
Road Workers, April 1882
Staatliche Museen zu Berlin, Berlin

(right)
FIG. 7
George Hendrik Breitner
The Dam, Amsterdam, 1893-97
Stedelijk Museum, Amsterdam

FIG. 8
Vincent van Gogh
*La Barrière with Horse-drawn Trams,
Paris*, 1887
Van Gogh Museum, Amsterdam

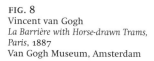

necessary skills and techniques kept him at a distance from established painters, and he forged friendships with the younger generation, Théophile de Bock, Herman van der Weele and George Hendrik Breitner.[14] It was the latter who took van Gogh on Zolaesque sketching trips at night around the slum districts of The Hague, notably de Geest. Both did drawings or watercolours of the poor, huddled outside soup kitchens or the lottery (FIGS. 4 & 5). Van Gogh's most ambitious, if still unresolved, composition of the period was a scene of workers laying gas pipes in the street – a scene of constructive disorder, physical labour and urban change that anticipated Breitner's later paintings of urban rebuilding in Amsterdam (FIG. 6, CAT. 48). The striking parallels between the work of these two products of Dutch art in the transitional period of the 1880s can be discerned in another shared aspect of city life, which was later explored away from The Hague: horse-drawn trams that Breitner painted in his *The Dam, Amsterdam:* 1893–97 (FIG. 7) and van Gogh in watercolour in his *Paris: La Barrière with Horse-drawn Tramway*, 1887 (FIG. 8).

The Netherlands had experienced a major political and economic revolution in the seventeenth century, which led to their mercantile and commercial pre-eminence as a trading nation that was signalled in elegant cities. But the Seven Provinces had suffered economic stagnation and political domination in the early part of the nineteenth century. The development of industry occurred much later than in most other European countries, really only taking off in the 1870s, when it caused extremes of poverty and rural emiseration. Even their railway system had to be developed by foreign capital. One of the major nineteenth-century collectors of the works of Dutch artists of the Hague School was James Staats Forbes, who was a British railway manager. He became familiar with the still traditional Dutch landscape and its painters when he was in the Netherlands overseeing the financial recovery of the Hollandsche Rijnspoor (Dutch Rhine Railway), which would bring many visitors and tourists to Dutch sea resorts. In Paul Gabriël's *In the Month of July, 1888* (CAT. 38) scudding clouds in a vast expanse of sky are reflected in the tranquil waters of the traditional forms of rural transport, the canal, which also carries the image of a premechanized windmill. We need to contrast this quintessential tourist vision of Holland as a rich agricultural landscape with a painting by Gabriël, *Train in a Landscape*, 1887 (FIG. 9). This painting uncomfortably juxtaposes a fisherman beside a canal with the noise and pollution of a railway train steaming down a line that runs beside an old canal, which is also marked out by unsightly telegraph poles. Such collisions of the technologically new and the traditional are rare in the art of the Hague School.[15] They remind us, however, that whatever we are shown in any painting derives its meaning from what the selected view and its manner of representation may neither acknowledge nor reveal.

FIG. 9
Paul Gabriël
Train in a Landscape, c. 1887
Rijksmuseum
Kröller-Müller, Otterlo

Paul Gabriël
In the Month of July
c. 1888
[CAT. 38]

George Hendrik Breitner
In the Dunes
(Horse Artillery), 1885–86
Early in his career, Breitner
was especially interested in
military subjects. These
artillery horsemen were
called the Yellow Riders (*Gele
Rijders*). Breitner exhibited
this painting in 1886 at the
Exhibition of Living Masters,
where it was enthusiastically
reviewed. The Rijksmuseum
purchased the work for 600
guilders, a rare acquisition
of contemporary art by the
institution.
[CAT. 44]

46

On the Beach

This leads me to two paintings in the exhibition: *Fishing Pinks in the Breakers,*
c. 1875–85, by Hendrik Willem Mesdag and Anton Mauve's *Morning Ride on the
Beach,* 1876 (CATS. 26 & 28 respectively).

Mesdag was born in Groningen, a substantial commercial city in the north
of the Netherlands from which Jozef Israëls also came. Married to the painter
Sientje van Houten, whose inheritance of a substantial fortune in 1866
enabled her husband to give up his job as a banker to become a full-time
artist, Mesdag was the cousin of Lawrence Alma-Tadema, who gave him an
introduction to the Brussels-based landscape artist Willem Roelofs. Van Gogh
would also later consult Roelofs in 1880.[16] In 1869 Mesdag moved to The
Hague to be near the village of Scheveningen, from which he could
daily paint the North Sea. In 1870 he built himself a house to accommodate
his growing collection of radically simplified oil sketches and paintings by an
older generation of French painters associated with the village of Barbizon –
hailed at the time as both the inheritors of the seventeenth-century Dutch
tradition of landscape painting and the artistic initiators of a new intimacy
with rural life and natural phenomena.[17] Mesdag's collection favoured the

most radically reduced, minimal and technically daring works of painters, whose much more complete Salon paintings themselves had been critically decried for abandoning the academic standards of finish, composition, drawing and colouration. This collection of French oil sketches anticipate some of the radical simplifications and painterly daring that Mesdag's Dutch colleagues in the Hague School would soon exhibit in their own works.

Mesdag's favoured subject was the sea and the fisher families who depended and laboured on it. To a landscape painter, this subject offered both the challenge of capturing within a narrow band of tonality the white-capped breakers of the North Sea, under its often sombre rain-filled skies, and the interest, for a figure painter, of the representation of bodies toughened by labour and spirits depressed by hardship. In Mesdag's paintings, large horizontal planes of sky and sea were punctuated by the masts, rigging and pinions of broad-bottomed fishing boats. At the end of the day, tired ponies would drag the boats onto the beach, where anxious families awaiting the return of the fishermen were ready to process the catch in their heavy baskets. Huddled groups of women in wooden clogs, whose sombre clothes of worn browns and reds were topped by white caps, are set among the intricate shapes of the rigged boats, some still heaving on the rough seas.

In 1880 Hendrik Mesdag was commissioned to paint a view of the village of Scheveningen for a panorama. A popular form of entertainment, the panorama was a vast circular painting housed in its own building, complete with a false foreground of real sand and derelict fishing tackle. The panorama was taken from the high point of Seinpostduin (Signpost dune), which afforded a view of the fishing boats on the beach, artillery exercising among

Jozef Israëls
Children of the Sea, 1872
Although Israëls often painted the hardships of Dutch fishermen, this painting, made shortly after he settled permanently in The Hague, shows an altogether happier seaside subject.
[CAT. 16]

48

Anton Mauve
Morning Ride on the Beach,
1876
One of the artist's most
famous works, this beach
scene was owned by James
Staats Forbes, London, one
of the greatest collectors
of Hague School paintings.
At one time, it was erro-
neously believed that the
two riders were Willem III
and Queen Emma.
[CAT. 28]

them, the village of Scheveningen, the distant spires of The Hague, and the
newly built summer villas and hotels of the burgeoning tourist industry. The
picturesque aspects of the fishing trade attracted tourists while threatening
it with the crowds of bathers and holidaymakers brought to the coast by expanding railways that linked the Dutch coast with Germany (FIG. 10). There
was a poignancy as well as a protest in choosing to represent the scene from
this famous dune, since this old landmark was destined to be levelled for the
building of a café-restaurant to further the appeal of this increasingly fashionable holiday resort.[18]

As the viewer of the panorama followed the circle of vision, she or he
would encounter that leisure aspect of the beach captured by Anton Mauve's
Morning Ride on the Beach or by George Breitner's *In the Dunes (Horse Artillery),*
1885–86 (CAT. 44).[19] (Breitner was one of Mesdag's young assistants on the
panorama.) Mauve's scintillating beach scene evokes the sunny brilliance of
the early morning, which renders the vast expanse of sand a glistening field
of brightness against which the silhouettes of elegant horses and riders create intriguing and fashionable shapes; they move through the dunes while

49

the distant sea almost merges into a flat sky. We can also just make out the bathing huts on the beach that await the arrival of the vacationing crowds.

Van Gogh visited the Mesdag Panorama in August 1881 and found it "deserves all respect." He was accompanied by one of its artists, Théophile de Bock, whose studio he also saw. On this same trip van Gogh had called on Anton Mauve for advice. He went to an exhibition of the Dutch Drawing Society (Hollandsche Teeken-maatschappij), where he saw "coloured drawings" by Jozef Israëls (a watercolour of the famous *Sewing Class at Katwijk*, now in the Taft Museum, Toledo), Jacob Maris (*A Mill in the Snow*), Anton Mauve (*Sheep in the Dunes* and *A Plough*) and works by Hendrik Mesdag and Jan Hendrik Weissenbruch. He met Willem Maris at de Bock's studio and was also given further advice on the development of his own drawings by Johannes Bosboom.

In December 1881 van Gogh came to live and work in The Hague. In his drawings, watercolours and early oil paintings (a range itself indicative of the Hague School's revival of watercolour, a medium made famous by late eighteenth-century British artists but otherwise disregarded by professional artists), we can see how van Gogh tried to work with all the diverse elements of the surroundings of the city of The Hague that had been encapsulated in the Mesdag Panorama, itself a reflection of the many threads present in the work of the artists associated with the Hague School: work, leisure, weather, and the picturesque. Van Gogh tried out his still uncertain watercolour technique on the fashionable crowds at leisure on Scheveningen's beaches and his incipient oil painting on a study of the return of the boats (FIG. 11). Van Gogh's student work shows us the complexity of this modernizing site, condensed into a chaotic and confusing range of possibilities. This stretch of sand was both the place of traditional lives and labours of the fishing community and the most modern of practices, leisure. These socioeconomic differences necessitated and dictated distinct means of representing the scene – from a range of finely calibrated tonalities in oils that conveyed the grim but determined character of rural life at the often stormy shore in contrast to the use of brighter colours and intense luminosity to evoke the attractions of summer at the seaside or the dashing elegance and verve of the military. A different palette and distinctly modern stylistic novelties were required for representing the leisure enjoyed by the bourgeoisie in contrast to the use of solid colours and drier, more impasted paint for conveying the stoic endurance of the labouring classes, who were tied to nature's resources and at the mercy of its unpredictability.

In a letter written in the early summer of 1883 to Anton van Rappard, van

FIG. 11
Vincent van Gogh
Beach at Scheveningen in Calm Weather,
1882
Van Gogh Museum, Amsterdam

Gogh discussed a series of drawings that he was currently making of gangs of workmen digging in the dunes for the sand that would be used for new roads being laid out as the city of The Hague expanded beyond its former boundaries (FIG. 12). The subject was not uncommon: we know examples by both Mauve (*The Sandpit*, 1879; watercolour, Haags Gemeentemuseum, The Hague) and by his other pupil, Herman van der Weele.[20] Van Gogh was not yet skilled enough to handle a composition of active, labouring figures within a convincing landscape setting. His failure, however, allows us to appreciate the skill involved in creating images of compelling simplicity, which were the hallmark of the older generation of the Hague School. For them even dynamic labour could be represented as part of an overall stillness through an almost imperceptible flattening and emphasis on the silhouette.

Van Gogh showed his work to Herman van der Weele, but the latter found van Gogh's drawings overcrowded and utterly without compositional value. Van der Weele's recommendations are very revealing: he suggested that van Gogh should dispense with the group of workers and focus on "one little fellow with his wheelbarrow on the dyke against the bright sky at sunset."[21] Radical simplification was a trait of Mauve's art – the eradication of distracting detail favoured a distillation of the feeling of the subject, which would be carried by the simple juxtaposition of an evocative evening landscape (made in oil or watercolour of poetically harmonized greys) with a single figure. The viewer could identify with this figure, but only at a generalizing distance where his hardship would be suitably softened into an evocative shape. Examples include Mauve's *The Tow Path* (National Gallery of Scotland, Edinburgh) and *The Shell Fish Gatherer* (Musée du Louvre, Paris). The human and his environment in which he laboured – but by which he was contained and even dwarfed – would be connected by pictorial bonds made all the more evident because other possibilities of the relation were erased in tonal harmonies and painterly washes. A group of workers defined by detailed draughtsmanship, such as van Gogh attempted, would make visible and thus unavoidable, issues of social relations, economic enterprise, change, the exploitation of raw materials for new social purposes, and the condition of the worker.

The model that van der Weele was advocating appears as simply good advice to an apprentice artist for making picturesque images of the burdens of labour. Yet, I suggest, that it encoded the Hague School's ideologically weighted vision about the very questions van Gogh seemed to be addressing – work and modernity – that displaces modern forms of collective work in favour of an image of a traditional bond between the human and the land-

Anton Mauve
The Marsh, 1885
The painting was produced shortly after Mauve left
The Hague to settle in Laren, in the Gooi region.
[CAT. 29]

scape that is nostalgically invented to represent the very opposite of moderni-ty. Such simplicity that could invest the quality of light, clouds, water, the tonalities of the earth and vegetation with poetic effect was one of the hall-marks of Anton Mauve's landscape painting and watercolours. His judicious and gradually acquired mastery over a reduced palette and expressive brush-work would produce the melancholic, even romantic image *The Marsh*, 1885 (CAT. 29). This pure landscape does not outwardly imitate the work of one of the most famous seventeenth-century landscape painters Jacob Ruysdael, but it does correspond with the mood projected onto his painting by nineteenth-century interpreters, who were themselves influenced by the Romantic move-ment that imagined the landscape as a projective mirror for emotions. Van Gogh would later try his hand at just such emotionally ladened skies, marsh-es and desolate vegetation when he was painting in Drenthe in 1883.

In 1881–82, however, van Gogh's attempt to make sense of the city led him in the exactly the opposite direction to that which van der Weele was point-ing him: namely, the direction being explored by George Hendrik Breitner. In place, therefore, of a way of painting that predisposes the viewer to experi-ence the scene or setting empathetically, imagining the mood created by the autumnal melancholy of a landscape or the human pain of a scene of bereave-ment, the younger generation zoomed in on details in order to observe the strange and unpredictable character of urban encounters or the disjointed-ness of a terrain undergoing economic transformation.

Making Sense of the Countryside, Multiculturally

After less than two years in The Hague, grappling with all that was on offer in this artistic centre, van Gogh left for the countryside, first in the peat fields of Drenthe and then in the southern province of Brabant where he had been raised. This move might appear retrograde, as if he were abandoning the modernity of the city, with which he was not yet able to work artistically. Yet in the next two years, we can see how van Gogh set aside what he had been trying out with Breitner, the better to grasp the lessons of the figure painters among his Hague School elders. Van Gogh's major work of his next period was a figure painting of peasants at their meal-time (*The Potato Eaters*), a subject central to the work of Jozef Israëls (*Midday Meal*, 1885, Dordrechts Museum, Dordrecht).

Israëls is significant not only as a Dutch artist, but as an artist from the Jewish community. The newly liberated Protestant Netherlands had been a place of settlement for the Spanish and Portuguese exiles since the sixteenth century, and major Jewish communities existed in The Hague, Groningen,

Jozef Israëls
A Scene of Life in Laren, 1905
[CAT. 18]

and especially Amsterdam, whose Jewish quarter had been represented by Rembrandt during the seventeenth century. It was, however, only in the nineteenth century that civil emancipation and the assimilation of the Jewish middle class to modern European society opened up professional possibilities, including artistic practice for artists such as Jozef Israëls. He was followed by his son Isaac, also an artist and fellow member of the Amsterdam School with George Breitner.

Jozef Israëls was born in Groningen to an observant and traditional Jewish family; he was destined for the rabbinate. In fact, he was sent into business, where he regularly visited Mesdag's father's offices before being allowed in 1840 to go to Amsterdam to study art. In his later paintings of the fishing communities at Zandvoort and Katwijk, Jozef Israëls, who had also trained in Paris (1845-47) in the academic tradition of Romantic history painting, began to treat grand themes of bereavement and tragedy as large-scale figure compositions, for example, *Passing Mother's Grave*, 1856 (Stedelijk Museum, Amsterdam) or *Fishermen Carrying a Drowned Man*, 1861 (National Gallery, London). His *Children of the Sea*, 1872 (CAT. 16) shows a more beneficent view of the ocean on which these children's fathers and mothers laboured so dangerously.

It is clear that as a painter Israëls had a considerable range in his palette and painterly styles. Yet, from the 1880s, he increasingly focused on a sombre palette, coupled with a colourist's freedom in his brushwork that harmonized his attention to the desolation of hard labour for meagre rewards with his concern to make his viewer engage emotionally with the courage of those living at the edges of economic survival, when they suffered the anguish of loss and solitude.

It might be important, therefore, to reappraise Israëls' seemingly idyllic, prettified images of family life in the cottages of the peasantry (CAT. 18) and his still poetic evocations of perhaps a more authentic destitution. They represent a negotiation, as an artist imbued with his own Jewish tradition, within the growing taste for rural genre painting, of opportunities for inscribing the great value attached to family relations, and the mother/child bond in Jewish culture.[22]

Israëls continued to explore the painful aspects of old age, loneliness and mourning, for instance, in *Growing Old* (Haags Gemeentemuseum, The Hague). He uses a deep chiaroscuro and sombre palette that drew upon Rembrandt, whose reputation was just being re-established in art historical circles. In the eighteenth century, Rembrandt had been dismissed as a dismal painter of sketchy effects and low subject matter. He was only elevated as a national

FIG. 13
Jozef Israëls
The Jewish Wedding, 1903
Rijksmuseum, Amsterdam

hero in the Netherlands after 1852, when the first statue was erected in his honour in Amsterdam. Art historians of the right attributed to his work a humanitarian spirituality, while those on the left saw in his unadulterated realism the model for a new, democratic *modern* art.[23] Israëls' contemporary, indeed quite radical homage to Rembrandt, can be detected in one of his self-conscious "Jewish" paintings, the celebration of his daughter's marriage in *The Jewish Wedding* (FIG. 13), a modern day version of Rembrandt's by then famous and admired *The Jewish Bride* (Rijksmuseum, Amsterdam). Van Gogh wrote about this painting on his visit to Amsterdam's museums in 1885:

> *Bürger [Thoré's pseudonym] has written about Rembrandt's* Jewish Bride...*surpassing himself....* The Jewish Bride, *not ranked so high, what an intimate, what an infinitely sympathetic picture it is, painted* d'une main de feu. *In* The Syndics *Rembrandt is true to nature, though even there, and always he soars aloft, to the very highest height, the infinite; but Rembrandt could do more than*

Jozef Israëls
David Playing the Harp,
1899
This is a preparatory oil
sketch for a large painting
of *Saul and David* made in
1899 (Stedelijk Museum,
Amsterdam).
[CAT. 17]

Vincent van Gogh
Self-Portrait, 1887
The painting was
produced during
the artist's sojourn
in Paris from
1886 to 1888.
[CAT. 42]

*that – if he did not have to be literally true, as in a portrait, when he was free to
idealize, to be a poet, that means a creator. That's what he is in* The Jewish
Bride. *...Rembrandt is so deeply mysterious that he says things for which there are
no words in any language. Rembrandt is truly called a magician.*[24]

On this same visit Van Gogh admired Israëls' *Fisherman of Zandvoort* and a
painting of "an old woman huddled together like a bundle of rags near the
bedstead in which the corpse of her husband lies." Israëls' series of biblical
paintings, such as *David Playing the Harp* (CAT. 17), link his address to contemporary Jewish life with a life-long interest in his Jewish heritage. Israëls' paintings of charitable institutions that tried to protect impoverished girls and the
aged formed a common concern with Thérèse Schwartze (*The Amsterdam
Orphanhouse*, 1885, Rijksmuseum, Amsterdam) and another major Jewish
artist, the Berlin-based Max Liebermann, who was so drawn to Dutch subjects
and their painters that he spent his summers in the Netherlands painting
within the Dutch school's ambit. Van Gogh was also to explore the subject of
the aged, urban poor during his period in The Hague.

Portraits of the Artist as a Dutch Dandy
Van Gogh is well known for the remarkable series of self-portraits that tempt
so many to read into these images his tortured autobiography. Placing the
artist's images within his Dutch context allows us to see this series as part of
its exploration of this modern identity. We have already discussed Thérèse
Schwartze's *Self-Portrait* (FIG. 2) and her portrait of the artist Lizzy Ansingh
(CAT. 64). George Hendrik Breitner used himself repeatedly as a model, painting images that served as manifestoes of both his well-known dandyism and
his painterly experiments. There are at least four major self-portraits from
the years of his close contact with van Gogh executed with a painterly verve
and an utterly original approach to the modernization of this image of creative masculinity: *Self-Portrait with Cigarette*, 1882 (Museum Boymans van
Beuningen, Rotterdam), *Self-Portrait with Lorgnette*, 1882–83 (Haags
Gemeentemuseum, The Hague, inscribed *à mon ami H.J. vd Weele*) and *Self-
Portrait*, 1882–83 (Art Gallery, Johannesburg).[25] The most daring is his *Self-
Portrait in the Studio* (FIG. 14). The cropped figure and low viewpoint create an
ironic address to the viewer, which we also find, although less daringly
framed, in Anton Mauve's *Self-Portrait*, c. 1888 (Haags Gemeentemuseum, The
Hague) – painted the very year that van Gogh engaged in a series of self-portrait exchanges with the young French artists working in Pont-Aven with
whom he was now affiliated, Emile Bernard and Paul Gauguin. It was also the

same year van Gogh was painting his homage to his recently deceased master in the form of a blossoming fruit tree, *Souvenir de Mauve*, 1888 (Rijksmuseum Vincent van Gogh, Amsterdam).

Van Gogh's *Self-Portrait* (CAT. 42) does not belong to the Dutch period of his work, nor yet to his oblique involvement in the Pont-Aven group. In this image the artist declared his allegiance to the art world, portraying himself as a Parisian dandy – dapper in his smart suit and grey felt hat. These garments replaced the peasant's smock or sheepskin that he had worn in Nuenen, the village in Brabant where he had spent the two years being "a painter of peasants."

Van Gogh's brief career as an artist between 1880 and 1890 was complicated by a series of moves from city to countryside, and country to country that themselves implied rapid shifts in what was the focus of his program for modern art. His alternating explorations of modernity in urban scenes and in nostalgia for the traditions of rural life and landscape corresponded with patterns that were equally present in the metropolitan avant-garde of Paris to which he became attached after 1886. Significantly, as we have seen, such shifting concerns with both the new versus the timeless, the modern versus the pre-modern, were also characteristic of the contemporary Dutch cultural scene from which he emerged and in which he had claimed in 1881 to be "rooted."

FIG. 14
George Hendrik Breitner
Self-Portrait in the Studio, c. 1888
Haags Gemeentemuseum,
The Hague

Rooted in Memories: The Homeland of Pictures

Van Gogh remained imaginatively attached not only to his Dutch origins through memories of childhood landscapes and experiences, but through a developing artistic program that was founded in the new art historical appreciation of the art of an older Holland – the paintings of Jacob Ruysdael, Jan van Goyen, Meindert Hobbema, Johannes Vermeer, and Rembrandt van Rijn.[26] In 1888 van Gogh wrote to his brother Theo (c. 19 July 1888) from Arles in the South of France: "Involuntarily – is it the effect of this country so reminiscent of Ruysdael? Here I think so often of Holland and across the twofold remoteness of distance and time gone by these memories have a kind of heartbreak in them."[27]

Van Gogh's art can provide a frame through which to consider more than the histories of individual artists' careers, stylistic movements or groupings in Dutch art that correspond with those at play across European culture in the nineteenth century: Romanticism, Realism, Naturalism, Symbolism, and so on. His art makes us ask questions: Why do forms of art change? Why do artists feel the need to reconsider how they put a painting together or even how they apply paint, how they represent space, or what they look at? Why do some artists find what they need in returning to past formulae while others discover the new precisely by breaching all existing conventions? Posing these same questions in the context of French painting between 1870 and 1890, art historian Meyer Schapiro argued that: "The broad reaction against existing art is only possible on the grounds of its inadequacy to artists with new values and new ways of seeing." Already in 1937, Schapiro challenged the exclusively formal interpretation of stylistic changes associated with French modernism by suggesting that the explanation for any new values and ways of seeing must lie in historical circumstances: "But the reaction in this internal, antithetical sense, far from being an inherent and universal property of culture, occurs only under impelling historical circumstances."[28] The impelling circumstances were what we call modernity, which had its own trajectory through the cities and countrysides of Holland, soliciting from its numerous artists in their informal groupings and creative disagreements a range of pictorial responses and, ultimately, in the work of Breitner and the Amsterdam school, a major examination of the core of modernity: the city and its populations, its spaces, its exchanges and its shocks. If van Gogh left Brabant for Paris while Breitner went to Amsterdam, the study of both their œuvres will benefit from our recognition that they were on a shared track. The artists of nineteenth-century Holland should not need van Gogh or Mondrian to remind us of their existence. But both these modern masters need a Dutch context for any serious understanding of their works.

Jacob Maris
The Truncated Windmill, 1872
This view of a windmill and bridge could be seen from Jacob Maris's studio
in The Hague. His brother later recalled that Jacob painted windmills from his window,
which may partly explain the cut-off view. A year later, the artist made a more
conventional view of the same scene (page 16).
[CAT. 33]

J. H. Weissenbruch
Autumn Landscape, c. 1885
Possessing a nervous shimmer typical of the artist, this
painting probably depicts a scene from the area around the
village of Noorden, near the Nieuwkoop lakes.

[CAT. 23]

Epilogue

Jacob Maris is represented in this exhibition by three paintings: one is a seascape entitled *The Truncated Windmill* (CAT. 33, reproduced on p. 60), which belongs with similar works by Mesdag and Mauve. It is an important work of the early 1870s, painted shortly after Maris arrived in The Hague from Paris and began to produce innovative views of the locality in which he lived – backstreets, vegetable gardens and canals. It was in these paintings that Maris tried out the dry, scumbled paint surfaces and limited palette of sombre browns and dulled greens that he might have seen exhibited in landscape painting in Paris. During the 1860s he had made a living in Paris by painting genre scenes for van Gogh's erstwhile employers, Goupil & Cie. Maris's work brought the Barbizon painters into the heart of the Hague School – and yet this canvas shows the radical exploration of the horizontal, the cropped, the combination of Holland's geometries of canal and fence, with the huddled shapes of cottage and the distinctive verticals of the windmill. No prettiness renders this scene picturesque, and when van Gogh turned to this quintessential Dutch landscape in The Hague, some of his more successful essays find whatever form and modern effect they achieve in a studied reflection of Jacob Maris's work of the early 1870s (FIG. 15).

FIG. 15
Vincent van Gogh
The Truncated Windmill
Christie's New York,
11 May 1989

NOTES

1. Van Gogh to Anton van Rappard, 15 October 1881, letter no. 2, *The Complete Letters of Vincent van Gogh*, 3 vols. (New York: Graphic Books Society, 1957). The translations, transcriptions, dating and ordering of van Gogh's correspondence with his brother, Theo, his sister, Wilhelmina, his artist friends Anton van Rappard and Emile Bernard, are under major revision in an enormous project undertaken by the Van Gogh Museum to ensure that scholars have the most reliable documents at their disposal. Until this is completed, scholars are obliged to work with some caution in their use of van Gogh letters, which have so far served to support the myth of the suffering isolate van Gogh rather than to assist in a critical art historical study van Gogh, who was a complex figure in the criss-crossing streams of nineteenth-century Dutch, British, German and French cultures.

2. The opening exhibition of New York's Museum of Modern Art in 1929 was the decisive moment for establishing this ortho-doxy, which became mainstream art history through John Rewald, *Post-Impressionism: From Van Gogh to Gauguin* (New York, Museum of Modern Art, 1956).

3. One of the major novels that signaled a new self-con sciouness in Dutch literature in the nineteenth century is *Max Havelaar*, written by Multatuli (Eduard Douwes Dekker) and pub-lished in 1860. The novel is a bitterly ironic critique of Dutch colo-nialism.

4. See Griselda Pollock, "Van Gogh and Holland: Nationalism and Modernism," *Dutch Crossing: Journal of Low Country Studies*, no. 44 (1991): 18-44.

5. J.H. van Eikeren, *De Amsterdamse Joffers* (Bussum, 1957).

6. For a discussion of women, work, politics, motherhood, prostitution, and modernity in Dutch culture, see Liesbeth Brandt Corstius et al., *De kunst van het moederschap: leven en werk van Nederlandse vrouwen in de 19e eeuw*, Nijmegen: Socialistische Uitgeverij, 1981. For its pertinence to van Gogh studies, see Carol Zemel, *Sisterhood: The Story of Wilhelmina van Gogh* (Amsterdam: Van Gogh Museum, 1997).

7. The model has been identified as Lise Jordan, the sister of Breitner's wife, both of whom modelled for the Amsterdam group of painters. Willem Witsen's photographic portrait of Lise Jordan wearing a veiled hat was probably used by Breitner for the paint-ing. Rieta Bergsma, "Fotograaf en Schilder," in *G.H. Breitner: fotograaf en schilder van het Amsterdamse stadgezicht*, ed. Anneka van Veen (Bussum: Thoth, 1997): 36-7.

8. T.J. Clark, *The Painting of Modern Life: Paris in the Art of Manet and His Followers* (New York: Alfred Knopf; London: Thames & Hudson, 1984); Griselda Pollock, "'The 'View from Elsewhere': Extracts from a Semi-Public Correspondence about the Visibility of Desire," in *Twelve Views of Manet's 'Bar'*, ed. Bradford Collins (Princeton: Princeton University Press, 1996): 278-314.

9. *Charles Baudelaire: A Lyric Poet in the Age of High Capitalism*, trans. Harry Zohn (London: Verso Books, 1973): 45.

10. See Griselda Pollock, "Modernity and the Spaces of Femininity," *Vision and Difference* (London: Routledge, 1988): 50-90.

11. Tineke de Ruiter, "Tussen Dynamiek en Verstilling," in *G.H. Breitner: fotograaf en schilder van het Amsterdamse stadgezicht, op. cit.*, 11-29.

12. See Ann Murray, "Strange and Subtle Perspective.... Van Gogh, the Hague School and the Dutch Landscape Tradition," *Art History* vol. 3, no. 4 (1980): 410-24.

13. Among the commercial and professional urban middle classes, there was a growing demand for images of "Nature," which was served by artists working in artistic colonies across the picturesque regions of Scandinavia, Brittany, Cornwell in England, and many parts of the Netherlands: Zandvoort, Katwijk, Drenthe, Laren. Some favoured the drama of confronting the untamed elements on the coast; others wanted to feel the recre-ative immersion in natural forms through forest scenes. Yet oth-ers fancied the difference of regional costume, climates and cus-toms as an access to a purer, more basic life. Holland offered some of these qualities, but contained within the picture of a regulated and once rich agricultural-mercantile social system. On artistic colonies and their concept of Nature, see Nina Lübbren, "Artists' Colonies in Europe," (Ph.D. diss., University of Leeds, 1996).

14. On van Gogh and the Hague School, see Griselda Pollock, "Vincent van Gogh and Dutch Art" (Ph.D. diss., University of London, 1980); Griselda Pollack, *Kijk op stad en land: Vincent van Gogh en zijn tijdgenoten 1870-1890* (Amsterdam: Rijksmuseum Vincent van Gogh, 1980); and Charles Moffett, "Van Gogh and the Hague School," in *The Hague School: Dutch Masters of the Nineteenth Century*, Ronald de Leeuw et al. (London: Weidenfeld and Nicolson, 1983): 137-146.

15. See for another much later example, H. Mesdag, *The New Harbour Construction at Enkhuizen*, 1905, The Hague, Mesdag Museum, no. 228.

16. See van Gogh to Theo, letter nos. 138, 141, 142, *Complete Letters*, for van Gogh's short-lived contacts with Roelofs in Brussels, when he may have had some lessons on perspective from Roelofs.

17. *Catalogue des Collections du Musée Mesdag: L'école française XIX siècle* (The Hague: Staatsuitgeverij, 1964). Mesdag collected works by Daubigny, Rousseau, Dupre, Millet, Michel, Corot.

18. John Sillevis, "The Heyday of the Hague School 1870-1885," in *The Hague School: Dutch Masters of the 19th Century*, ed. Ronald de Leeuw (London: Weidefeld and Nicolson, 1983): 85.

19. On the modernity of the military man, see Charles Baudelaire, "The Painter of Modern Life" [1863] in *The Painter of Modern Life and Other Essays*, ed. Jonathan Mayne (Oxford: Phaidon Press, 1964): 24-26. It is thought that Breitner used contemporary photographs, which for the first time revealed to the human eye the specific character of a horse's combinations of four legs in dif-ferent gaits.

20. *Sanddigging*, oil on canvas, D. Bolten, The Hague. For more examples, see Anna Wagner, *Schilders zien de duinen* (The Hague: 1974).

21. Van Gogh to Anton van Rappard, letter no. 37, *Complete Letters*.

22. In our century Josef Hermann, an artist who survived the Holocaust, found himself at home painting and drawing the min-ers in the Welsh valleys because, he states, he found in their hard lives lived within tradition and religion an echo of his lost Jewish world from Eastern Europe. Monica Boh-Duchen, "A Jewish Artist among the Miners: Jozef Herman," *Jewish Quarterly*, no.170 (1998): 54-58.

23. Charles Blanc, the founding editor of the *Gazette des Beaux Arts*, published in 1859 a multi-volumed work entitled *Histoire des Peintres de Toutes les Ecoles* (1849-73), for which he wrote the volume on Dutch art (1861-68). He set Rembrandt up as the great religious painter in his two volumes on the artist: *L'Oeuvre de Rembrandt* (1853) and *L'Oeuvre Complet de Rembrandt* (1856, 1859, 1873, 1880). Théophile Thoré, a major innovator in the formation of documen-tary art history, published two volumes on *Les Musées de la Hollande* (1858-60). In his many publications he promoted the model of what he called the realism of Dutch art's accessible treatment of everyday life and actual people – portrait, landscape and genre painting – as the model for modern art. Van Gogh was deeply influenced by both writers. See Griselda Pollock, "Vincent van Gogh and Dutch Art" (Ph.D. diss., University of London, 1980), soon to be published as *The Case Against Van Gogh': The Cities and Countries of Modernism* (London: Thames and Hudson, 1999).

24. Van Gogh to Theo, October 1885, letter no. 426, *Complete Letters*.

25. For a comparable examination of the self-portrait and the politics of masculine creativity at the beginnings of German mod-ernism, see Irit Rogoff, "The Anxious Artist – Self-Portraits and Cultural Ideologies," in *The Divided Heritage: Themes and Problems in German Modernism* (Cambridge: Cambridge University Press, 1991).

26. Griselda Pollock, "On Not Seeing Provence: Van Gogh and the Landscape of Consolation, 1888-89," in *Framing France: The Representation of Landscape in France 1870-1914*, ed. Richard Thomson (Manchester and New York: Manchester University Press, 1998): 81-118.

27. Van Gogh to Theo, letter no. 512, *Complete Letters*.

28. Meyer Schapiro, "The Nature of Abstract Art," *Marxist Quarterly* (January-March 1937): 81; reprinted in Meyer Schapiro, *On Modern Art* (New York: George Braziller, 1979): 185-216.

Gerard Bilders
The Goat-herdess, c. 1864
[CAT. 13]

Catalogue of the Exhibition

WOUTER VAN TROOSTWIJK
Amsterdam 1782–1810 Amsterdam

1.
Gelderland Landscape, c. 1809
Canvas, 52.5 x 63 cm

PIETER GERARDUS VAN OS
The Hague 1776–1839 The Hague

2.
A Watercourse near 's-Graveland, 1818
Canvas, 111.5 x 89.5 cm
Signed lower centre: *P. G. Van Os f 1818*

ANDREAS SCHELFHOUT
The Hague 1787–1870 The Hague

3.
Farmyard, 1828
Paper on canvas, 29 x 28 cm
Signed lower centre: *A. Schelfhout f.*

WIJNAND NUYEN
The Hague 1813–1839 The Hague

4.
Shipwreck on a Rocky Coast, c. 1837
Canvas, 154 x 206 cm
Signed lower left: *W. J. J. Nuijen Bz. f.*

BAREND CORNELIS KOEKKOEK
Middelburg 1803–1862 Kleve

5.
Winter Landscape, 1838
Canvas, 62 x 75 cm
Signed lower right: *B.C. Koekkoek f.*

JOHANNES TAVENRAAT
Rotterdam 1809–1881 Rotterdam

6.
The Storm, 1843
Wood, 31 x 39.8 cm
Signed lower left: *Tavenraat 1843*

CORNELIS SPRINGER
Amsterdam 1817–1891 Hilversum

7.
*View of The Hague from the Delftse Vaart
in the Seventeenth Century*, 1852
Canvas, 48 x 58 cm
Signed lower left: C. Springer

PIERRE LOUIS DUBOURCQ
Amsterdam 1815–1873 Amsterdam

8.
*Ripened Wheat, The Black Forest near
Baden-Baden*, 1855
Canvas, 154 x 206 cm
Signed lower right: *Dubourcq*

JOHAN BARTHOLD JONGKIND
Lattrop 1819–1891 La-Côte-Sainte-André

9.
View on a French River, 1855
Canvas, 24.3 x 32.4 cm
Signed lower left: *Jongkind 1855*

10.
Overschie in the Moonlight, 1871
Canvas, 22 x 27.5 cm
Signed lower right: *Jongkind 1871*

GERARD BILDERS
Utrecht 1838–1865 Amsterdam

11.
Meadow near Oosterbeek, c. 1860
Canvas, 39 x 55 cm
Signed lower right: *A.G. Bilders*

12.
Pond in the Woods at Sunset, c. 1862
Wood, 22 x 35 cm
Signed lower left: Gerard Bilders

13.
The Goat-herdess, c. 1864
Canvas, 61.5 x 53 cm
Signed lower left: *Gerard Bilders*

JAN WEISSENBRUCH
The Hague 1822–1880 The Hague

14.
A City Gate in Leerdam, before 1870
Canvas, 77 x 104 cm
Signed left: *JAN WEISSENBRUCH. F*

JOHANNES BOSBOOM
The Hague 1817–1891 The Hague

15.
Church Interior, 1848
Canvas, 56.7 x 41 cm
Signed lower centre: *J. Bosboom*

JOZEF ISRAËLS
Groningen 1824–1911 Scheveningen

16.
Children of the Sea, 1872
Canvas, 48.5 x 93.5 cm
Signed left: *Jozef Israels / 1872*

17.
David Playing the Harp, 1899
Canvas, 58.5 x 39.5 cm
Signed lower left: *Jozef Israels*

18.
A Scene of Life in Laren, 1905
Canvas, 132 x 103 cm
Signed lower left: *Jozef Israels*

WILLEM ROELOFS
Amsterdam 1822–1897 Berchem (near Antwerp)

19.
Landscape with Approaching Storm, 1850
Canvas, 90.2 x 139.8 cm
Signed lower left: *W. Roelofs f. 1850*

20.
Meadow Landscape with Cattle, c. 1870
Canvas, 49.2 x 77.3 cm
Signed lower left: *W. Roelofs*

21.
The Bridge on the Ijssel near Doesburg, 1889
Canvas mounted on wood, 24.5 x 45.5 cm
Signed lower left: *W. Roelofs / Doesborgh 1889*

J.H. WEISSENBRUCH
The Hague 1824–1903 The Hague

22.
*View near the Geestbrug: The Rijswijk
Shipping Canal*, 1868
Wood, 31 x 50 cm
Signed lower right: *J. Hendrik. Weissenbruch f 68*

23.
Autumn Landscape, c. 1885
Canvas, 41.3 x 66.5 cm
Signed lower right: *J. H. Weissenbruch f*

24.
The Basement of the Artist's House in The Hague,
1888
Canvas, 39 x 51 cm
Signed lower right: *J. H. Weissenbruch f 88*

25.
Forest near Barbizon, 1900
Canvas, 48.5 x 64 cm
Signed lower left: *Barbizon / J. H. Weissenbruch 1900*

HENDRIK WILLEM MESDAG
Groningen 1831–1915 The Hague

26.
Fishing Pinks in the Breakers, c. 1875–85
Canvas, 90 x 181 cm
Signed lower left: *H.W. Mesdag*

27.
Waves Battering a Lighthouse, c. 1890–95
Canvas, 52 x 40 cm
Signed lower left: *H.W.M [...]*

ANTON MAUVE
Zaandam 1838–1888 Arnhem

28.
Morning Ride on the Beach, 1876
Canvas, 45 x 70 cm
Signed lower right: *A. Mauve f.*

29.
The Marsh, 1885
Canvas, 60 x 90 cm
Signed lower left: *A. Mauve f.*

30.
The Vegetable Garden, c. 1887
Canvas, 61 x 87 cm
Signed lower right: *A. Mauve f.*

MATTHIJS MARIS
The Hague 1839–1917 London

31.
Small Boat near a Pollard Willow, 1863
Paper mounted on wood, 23 x 30 cm
Signed lower right: *MM63*

JACOB MARIS
The Hague 1837–1899 Karlsbad

32.
Feeding the Chickens, 1866
Canvas, 33 x 21 cm
Signed lower right: *J Maris fe 1866*

33.
The Truncated Windmill, 1872
Canvas, 45 x 112.5 cm
Signed lower right: *J Maris 1872*

34.
*Bluff-bowed Fishing Boat on the Beach
at Scheveningen*, c. 1880
Canvas, 101.5 x 89.5 cm
Signed lower right: *J. Maris*

WILLEM MARIS
The Hague 1844–1910 The Hague

35.
Cow Reflected in Water, c. 1885–95
Canvas, 65 x 81 cm
Signed lower left: *Willem Maris*

PAUL GABRIËL
Amsterdam 1828–1903 Scheveningen

36.
Landscape near Kortenhoef, 1877
Wood, 37 x 57.5 cm
Signed lower right: *Gabriël f. 77*

37.
A Watercourse near Abcoude, 1878
Wood, 41 x 50 cm
Signed lower right: *Gabriel f. 78*

38.
In the Month of July, c. 1888
Canvas, 102 x 66 cm

LAWRENCE ALMA-TADEMA
Dronrijp (Friesland) 1836–1912 Wiesbaden

39.
The Death of Pharaoh's First-born Son, 1872
Canvas, 77 x 124.5 cm
Signed upper centre: *L. Alma Tadema*

40.
The Egyptian Widow, 1872
Canvas, 75 x 99 cm
Signed lower centre: *L. Alma Tadema 1872*

VINCENT VAN GOGH
Zundert 1853–1890 Auvers-sur-Oise

41.
Village at Sunset, 1884
Canvas on cardboard, 57 x 82 cm

42.
Self-Portrait, 1887
Board, 42 x 34 cm

43.
Wild Roses, 1889
Canvas, 23.5 x 32 cm

GEORGE HENDRIK BREITNER
Rotterdam 1857–1923 Amsterdam

44.
In the Dunes (Horse Artillery), 1885–86
Canvas, 115 x 77.5 cm
Signed lower left: *G.H. Breitner*

45.
*View on the Oosterpark in Amsterdam
in the Snow*, 1891–92
Canvas, 70 x 122 cm

46.
Girl in a White Kimono (Geesje Kwak), 1894
Canvas, 59 x 57 cm
Signed upper left: *G. H. Breitner*

47.
*The Singelbrug at the Paleisstraat in
Amsterdam*, 1896–98
Canvas, 100 x 152 cm
Signed lower right: *G. H. Breitner*

48.
*Midday Break at a Building Site on the Van
Diemenstraat, Amsterdam*, c. 1898
Canvas, 78 x 115 cm
Signed lower left: *G. H. Breitner*

49.
Ships in the Ice, 1901
Canvas, 115 x 163 cm
Signed lower right: *G. H. Breitner*

50.
The Damrak, Amsterdam, c. 1903
Canvas, 100 x 150 cm
Signed lower left: *G. H. Breitner*

GEORGE POGGENBEEK
Amsterdam 1853–1903 Amsterdam

51.
The Willow, c. 1888
Board, 26 x 22 cm
Stamped lower right: *Atelier Geo. Poggenbeek*

52.
View of Dinan, c. 1895–96
Canvas mounted on wood, 33 x 50 cm
Signed lower left: *Geo Poggenbeek*

ISAAC ISRAËLS
Amsterdam 1865–1934 The Hague

53.
Two Girls in the Snow, c. 1890–94
Wood, 65 x 36 cm
Signed lower left: *ISAAC / ISRAELS*

54.
A Shop Window, c. 1894–98
Canvas, 59 x 64 cm
Signed lower left: *ISAAC / ISRAELS*

55.
Donkey-Riding on the Beach, c. 1898–1900
Canvas, 51 x 70 cm
Signed lower right: *ISAAC ISRAELS*

56.
In the Bois de Boulogne, *Paris*, c. 1906
Canvas, 33 x 46 cm
Signed lower right: *ISAAC / ISRAELS*

WILLEM WITSEN
Amsterdam 1860–1923 Amsterdam

57.
Winter Landscape, c. 1895
Canvas, 45 x 52 cm
Signed lower right: *Witsen.*

58.
Landscape with Fields, c. 1900–1905
Canvas, 33 x 66 cm

59.
Warehouses on the Uilenburg, Amsterdam, c. 1911
Canvas, 52 x 42 cm
Signed lower left: *Witsen.*

WILLEM DE ZWART
The Hague 1862–1931 The Hague

60.
Hackney Coaches, c. 1890–94
Canvas, 31.5 x 43 cm
Signed lower left: *W. de ZWART.*

GERRIT WILLEM DIJSSELHOF
Zwollerkerspel (Zwolle) 1866–1924 Bloemendaal

61.
Pike and Perch in an Aquarium, c. 1895–1900
Canvas, 100 x 100 cm
Monogrammed lower left: *GWD*

62.
Tulip Fields, c. 1905
Wood, 20 x 35 cm
Monogrammed lower left: *GWD*

JAN VETH
Dordrecht 1864–1925 Amsterdam

63.
Cornelia, Clara, and Johanna Veth:
The Artist's Three Sisters, 1884
Canvas, 88.5 x 108 cm

THÉRÈSE SCHWARTZE
Amsterdam 1851–1918 Amsterdam

64.
Portrait of Lizzy Ansingh, 1902
Canvas, 78 x 62 cm
Signed upper right: *Th. Schwartze. 1902.*

FLORIS VERSTER
Leiden 1861–1927 Leiden

65.
Anemones, 1888
Canvas, 90 x 46 cm
Signed upper right: *Floris Verster*

JAN TOOROP
Purworedjo (Indonesia) 1858–1928 The Hague

66.
The Sea at Katwijk, 1887
Canvas, 86 x 96 cm
Signed lower left: *J. Toorop 1887*

PIET MONDRIAN
Amersfoort 1872–1944 New York

67.
Still Life with Oranges, c. 1900
Canvas, 48 x 32 cm
Signed lower left: *P. MONDRIAAN*

68.
River View with a Boat, c. 1903
Canvas, 66 x 102 cm
Signed lower right: *P. MONDRIAAN*

Selected Bibliography

All the Paintings of the Rijksmuseum in Amsterdam: A Completely Illustrated Catalogue. Amsterdam: Rijksmuseum, 1976 [with a supplement, 1992].

Bionda, R., and C. Blotkamp, eds. *The Age of Van Gogh: Dutch Painting, 1880-1895* (exhibition catalogue). Glasgow: Burrell Collection; Amsterdam: Van Gogh Museum, 1990-91.

De Leeuw, R., J. Sillevis, and C. Dumas, eds. *The Hague School: Dutch Masters of the 19th Century* (exhibition catalogue). Paris: Grand Palais; London: Royal Academy of Arts; The Hague: Haags Gemeentemuseum, 1983.

Loos, W., and G. Jansen. *Breitner and His Age: Paintings from the Rijksmuseum in Amsterdam, 1880-1900.* Amsterdam: Rijksmuseum, 1995.

Loos, W., G. Jansen, and W. Kloek. *Waterloo, Before and After: Paintings from the Rijksmuseum in Amsterdam, 1800-1830.* Amsterdam: Rijksmuseum, 1997.

Loos, W., R.-J. te Rijdt, M. van Heteren et al. *On Country Roads and Fields: The Depiction of the 18th- and 19th-Century Landscape* (exhibition catalogue). Amsterdam: Rijksmuseum, 1997-98.

Vels Heijn, A. *South Wing: A New Museum within a Museum.* Amsterdam: Rijksmuseum, 1996.

Welsh-Ovcharov, Bogomila. *Vincent van Gogh and the Birth of Cloisonism* (exhibition catalogue). Toronto: Art Gallery of Ontario, 1981.

Acknowledgements

We are grateful to Wouter Kloek for his collaboration on this exhibition, and for the support of his colleagues at the Rijksmuseum, Guido Jansen, Marjon van Heteren, and Wim Hoeben. Warm thanks also to Sarah Head, D.J. van Houten, Mieke Bos, and Paul Schellekens.

Photographs

Copyright © Rijksmuseum, Amsterdam, and collections as indicated in captions.

Catalogue

Design: Bryan Gee
Typeface: Swift by Gerard Unger
Film and Printing: Bowne of Toronto

J.H. Weissenbruch
The Basement of the Artist's House in The Hague, 1888
[CAT. 24]